GW00838333

# The Allies
## *of*
# Humanity

◆

## BOOK FOUR

# The Allies
## *of*
# Humanity

◆

## BOOK FOUR

◆

### FREEDOM IN THE UNIVERSE

Marshall Vian Summers

# THE ALLIES OF HUMANITY BOOK FOUR: Freedom in the Universe

Copyright © 2019 by The Society for the New Message

All rights reserved. No part of this publication may be reproduced, stored in a retrieval system or transmitted in any form or by any means, electronic, mechanical, photo-copying, recording or otherwise without the prior written permission of the publisher.

*Edited by Darlene Mitchell*
*Book Cover: Designed by Tyyne Andrews*
*Book Interior: Designed by Reed Summers*

ISBN: 978-1-942293-97-2 (POD)
ISBN: 978-1-942293-98-9 (ebook)
NKL Version 7.6 : Sv7.3 6/12/19
Library of Congress Control Number: 2019907231


PUBLISHER'S CATALOGING-IN-PUBLICATION DATA
*(Prepared by The Donohue Group, Inc.)*

Names: Summers, Marshall Vian, author.
Title: The allies of humanity. Book four, Freedom in the universe /
    Marshall Vian Summers.
Other Titles: Freedom in the universe
Description: Boulder, CO : New Knowledge Library, the publishing imprint
    of The Society for the New Message, [2019] | "A New Message book."]
Identifiers: ISBN 9781942293972 (POD) | ISBN 9781942293989 (ebook)
Subjects: LCSH: Civilization--Extraterrestrial influences. | Extraterrestrial beings.
    | Human-alien encounters. | Liberty.
Classification: LCC CB156.S934 2019 (print) | LCC CB156 (ebook) |
    DDC 001.942--dc23

*The Allies of Humanity Book Four* is a book of the New Message from God and is published by New Knowledge Library, the publishing imprint of The Society for the New Message. The Society is a religious non-profit organization dedicated to presenting and teaching a New Message for humanity. The books of New Knowledge Library can be ordered at www.newknowledgelibrary.org, your local bookstore and at many other online retailers.

The New Message is being studied in more than 30 languages in over 90 countries. *The Allies of Humanity Book Four* is being translated into the many languages of our world by a dedicated group of volunteer student translators from around the world. These translations will all be available online at www.newmessage.org.


**The Society for the New Message**
P.O. Box 1724 Boulder, CO 80306-1724
(303) 938-8401 (800) 938-3891
011 303 938 84 01 (International) (303) 938-1214 (fax)
newmessage.org newknowledgelibrary.org
alliesofhumanity.org
email: society@newmessage.org

# CONTENTS

# A MESSAGE FROM
# MARSHALL VIAN SUMMERS

It is a great pleasure for me to present to you the fourth set of Briefings from the Allies of Humanity. These Briefings are part of a greater communication from those races in our local universe who support humanity's freedom and sovereignty as it emerges into a "Greater Community" of life. This is an authentic message from an extraterrestrial source, warning us of the dangers of Intervention from beyond and urging us to prepare for the challenges of life in the universe.

The Allies of Humanity are a group of individuals from several different worlds who came to the vicinity of the Earth to observe the alien Intervention that is occurring in our world and to report on the activities of this Intervention and its implications for the human race.

Through their Briefings, the Allies are revealing the reality of Contact occurring in the world today—who the visitors are, why they are here and the larger agenda behind their activities. In doing so, the Briefings fill in many of the critical gaps in our understanding of the reality of extraterrestrial visitation and the UFO phenomenon, which have been the focus of research and inquiry for over seven decades.

The Briefings provide us a clear picture of who we are encountering, what this means for humanity and how we can prepare for this—the greatest and most consequential event in human history. And yet these Briefings are also a gift, for they give us a window into the realities of life in our local region of space, a vision we could not have otherwise.

The Allies are not here on our planet influencing our governments, our science or our religions. Instead they came to the vicinity of our world to witness the Intervention taking place on Earth and to provide us a series of Briefings that reveal vital information about what is happening, why it is happening, what it means and what we must do to prepare. The Allies are not giving these Briefings to governments or people in positions of power. They are giving these Briefings to the people of our world.

The Allies contacted me in 1996 and presented their first set of Briefings in 1997 and 1998. This first set of Briefings was then published in the year 2000 as *The Allies of Humanity Briefings: An Urgent Message about the Extraterrestrial Presence in the World Today*. There was no further communication from the Allies in the two years that followed.

The Allies contacted me again in December of 2000 with a second set of Briefings. Under great duress, they revealed that after the publication of their first set of Briefings, they were identified and pursued by the Intervention and needed to convey their second set of Briefings immediately. All six Briefings were given in one day.

Eight years later, the Allies contacted me again with their third set of Briefings, now speaking from far beyond the world. All seven Briefings were given in one day in June 2008.

And then eight years later came the fourth set of Briefings. They were revealed to me in October 2016, with all six Briefings given in one day.

I cannot account for why there were such large periods of time between the Briefings. Perhaps it was the circumstances facing the Allies after they were forced to depart the vicinity of the Earth. Or perhaps there were greater events taking place beyond our world that involved the Allies' mission and those they represent.

All told, these Briefings present a body of understanding and perspective that we as human beings could not obtain ourselves, given at a time of critical need as the foreign presence of Intervention in the world grows and becomes ever more influential here in ways that we can barely understand. For humanity is unaware and unprepared for this great threshold: our encounter with intelligent life in the universe, which is occurring not from our journeys into space, but from the arrival of those who have come here for their own purposes.

I would like to give you an overview of the first three sets of Briefings and then speak about the fourth set of Briefings. The first three sets of Briefings reveal that humanity is not alone in the universe or even within our own world. With this, they reveal that there is an extraterrestrial presence in our world functioning here in a secretive manner affecting people worldwide.

This is an Intervention from aggressive forces in our local universe who are seeking to gain control of the world's resources for themselves. This is an Intervention from which we will not benefit and to which we will be subjected if we succumb to its persuasions.

Those intervening in our world want us to work for them, for they cannot live here. They cannot breathe our atmosphere; they cannot face the biological complexity of our world. They need us as part of the resources of the world. This is a process overall of intervention and colonization being undertaken over a long period of time, to be achieved without the use of force.

The Briefings tell us that the Intervention occurring in the world today means that our isolation in the universe is now over and that we will have to face contact from intervening forces well into the future. Protecting our world and our sovereignty will be an ongoing requirement into the future.

Why is Intervention happening now? The Intervention is here because we are degrading a world rich in resources that they want to control for themselves. The Intervention values the Earth and is watching us destroy and degrade it at a phenomenal pace. Here the Briefings tell us that the Earth is a prize desired by others in a universe of barren worlds. And Intervention is now proceeding because we have created a structure of commerce and communication that it can utilize for its own purposes.

Throughout their Briefings, the Allies talk about the importance of human freedom and self-determination in an environment of tremendously powerful persuasion and inducements, particularly cast upon a young race emerging into this Greater Community of life, and how many other emerging races in the universe have fallen prey to Intervention such as we are facing now.

We are unprepared for Contact with this Greater Community. For we can only imagine, through our media, film and science, what life might be like beyond our borders. But the picture that the Allies Briefings present is very different than what most people think of today.

The Allies Briefings are grounded in the realities of life in our local universe and therefore present a much more accurate representation of what actually exists beyond us. From this, we can begin to see that the universe is an expression of the same reality of nature that we experience in our world. Yet it is nature occurring on a scale and a level of complexity beyond what we can imagine.

As a result, the Allies Briefings emphasize that we can understand the reality of Intervention from our own experience of intervention here on Earth. Our history has shown us the evidence of intervention of one culture upon another, one nation upon another, repeatedly over time. This means that our own history and native wisdom can enable us to see and understand a great deal about who is here and why they have come.

Yet there is much we cannot see and know about what life is like in our local universe, but which we would need to know if we are to understand who is visiting our world. To understand who is here and why they're here and what this means for us, we have to understand something about what life is like in the universe around us. We have to understand what would bring an Intervention here, what creates it, what strengthens it, what gives it power, what limits its power. The first three sets of Allies Briefings provide us this perspective very directly.

The fourth set of Briefings builds upon this and focuses on freedom in the universe, how it is achieved, how it is maintained and the restraints humanity will have to adhere to in order to become a free race in the universe.

With this, they reveal the great Spiritual Coordination that exists throughout the universe through which the Creator of all life supports spiritual development, awareness, unity and freedom in the universe.

The Allies devote one of their Briefings to the Networks of the Wise, which represents individuals in many different worlds who are being guided by this Greater Coordination to support their world's freedom and well-being, creating a vast network through which wisdom can be sent from one world to another. The Allies reveal that they are part of this Network of the Wise.

Throughout their Briefings, the Allies emphasize that we are now the native peoples of the Earth, facing Intervention from powers from beyond. To recognize this requires courage, clarity, objectivity and awareness. The time for this awareness and recognition has come.

Our need is pressing and it is now. There are things we must know about life in the universe around us and about the nature and purpose of those intervening in our world today, which the Allies of Humanity are revealing to us.

The Allies of Humanity emphasize that we must resist the Intervention through education, through awareness building, and through a growing human alliance and the empowerment of those who are seeing the Intervention's activities and who are being affected by them.

To do this, the Allies emphasize that we must rely upon the power of our innate spiritual Intelligence within, which is called "Knowledge." This greater Intelligence is humanity's inherent ability to see and to know the truth beyond fear and preference, to see and know the Intervention for what it really is.

To enable us to gain access to this Knowledge, a preparation has been given to us from the Creator of all life called the Steps to Knowledge. This is the pathway of discovering Knowledge and building your connection to it in the context of the Greater Community.

Therefore, I welcome you and encourage you to explore these Briefings with an open mind, allowing your thoughts to be challenged, allowing old beliefs to be overturned if necessary, allowing something new and vital and necessary to be given to you as a person and to all of us together.

# Who We Are and What We Represent

We give greetings. We are the Allies of Humanity here to speak with you once again after a long delay. We are far away from your world now, and we have been away for some time. But there is much we can impart to you that will be of great significance and importance for your future and for the possibility of you growing and becoming a free race in the universe, where true freedom is so very rare.

We speak for those free races who live amongst many others who are not free. But we are not here representing their governments. Instead, we were sent by Higher Powers from the spiritual realm to give these Briefings to humanity.

We have come from several nations for this purpose and are united in our cause. You will not know our names nor the names of our worlds, for they must remain hidden. Once you begin to understand the realities of life in the

Greater Community in the universe, you will be able to understand why this discretion must be exercised.

You who broadcast everything out into space around you will have to realize that to be free, you must be discreet. This is a great lesson for humanity to learn as it stands at the threshold of a universe full of intelligent life.

We are here to give you counsel and perspective and to correct many of your assumptions or beliefs that could jeopardize your ability to understand your situation and the great challenge you now face from Intervention in your world from beyond by other races who are here to take advantage of your weakness, your divisions, and your superstitions for their own purposes—to establish their precedence in this world without the use of force.

We have spoken of this at great length in our previous Briefings. But now we must tell you about some other things that are important to know about the meaning of freedom in this universe—what it will mean for your world, the great change that it will bring to your understanding, and the greater unity it will require amongst your nations.

For you will not remain a free world if you continue your struggle with one another—your dissensions, your competition, your violence, your wars. Fighting amongst yourselves, you have no idea of the presence of those who are intervening, or the many eyes in your local universe who are watching you, and all the errors of humanity being broadcast out into space for the discreet observer to see—your tribes warring with one another in a beautiful world that is desired by others. And though there are not many other races or nations that are aware of your existence, the challenge is yet very great, very real and growing all the time.

So we must speak of things now that have to do with your future, that have to do with the possibility of humanity becoming a free race in a universe where competition has been carried to greater levels than you understand.

We give this with great respect for humanity because you have kept your religious traditions alive, and the power of Knowledge within the individual is still recognized and honored here, where it has been lost and forgotten or never realized in so many other places. For the great technological nations in your local region of space are largely devoid of religion, spirituality and the higher ethics that you may still hold dear, which we value as well.

You stand at the great turning point of whether you will fall into submission to foreign powers or whether you will rise up from your endless conflicts to establish yourself as a free nation. We have given much wisdom and perspective on this in our previous Briefings. But now we must tell you what freedom means and what it will require of your nations and your peoples.

While worlds are distinct and unique and different in many ways, the requirements of freedom in the universe are the same for all. You must understand these requirements and not neglect them in any way.

For peace amongst your nations is not merely the cessation of war and conflict. It must be a preparation for a greater engagement and a greater set of challenges that your world is facing now and will face increasingly as you go forward.

Your freedom now is to protect the world, to insulate the world from those powers that will all seek to intervene here, both through the physical environment and through the mental environment.

The freedom that will require your nations to be cooperative will also require that there cannot be great dissension, for the influence from the outside, from the Greater Community, will seek to stimulate dissension, as it is doing now. It will seek to weaken the strongest nations by engaging them in endless and intractable conflicts and competition. It will seek to weaken people's belief in their own governments and institutions, as is occurring now.

The strength of human leadership and institutions must become stronger in the future and more united between nations and across the nations. For what will unite humanity is the challenge of the Greater Community. What will require cooperation will be the threat of Intervention from beyond. What will elevate humanity in its unity and purpose is its emergence into this larger arena of intelligent life.

Freedom here is not the freedom to be chaotic or the freedom to break down into individualistic purpose and pursuits alone. It is the freedom to insulate and protect your world from the greater technological powers that exist around you, who will seek to persuade you and to divide you through subtle means.

For conquest is not allowed in this region of space. We have spoken of this at length before. Yet it must be repeated, for humanity is still very warlike and competitive in its attitude. It will think of Intervention in military terms. But no intervening race or group seeks to destroy the resources of this world or their hope that humanity will become a workforce—compliant and allegiant to them. You must now begin to think in new ways, for influence in the Greater Community is powerful. It is the threshold that is awaiting you now.

Your freedom in the future, should you be able to gain it and maintain it, will limit individual freedom out of necessity. For all the citizens of the world will have to be committed to the protection of the world. It will be fundamental. Though once you begin to see the tentacles of the Intervention, in the world today and in the future, this understanding will grow and must become part of your foundation.

You do not realize you live on a beautiful planet in a universe of barren worlds. Most habitation in worlds is a product of advanced technology, and the worlds of origin of advancing races have largely been despoiled, such as you are despoiling your world now.

It is a Greater Community awareness and understanding that we are advocating here today with you. You cannot think like primitive people, for the universe you are facing is not primitive. You cannot refer to the past only, except to understand that all Intervention is carried out for aggressive purposes. Think not that any race will come here to really help you, for if they establish their appearance here in a visible way, it will be part of a great persuasion.

If you degrade the world continually, you will become so unstable in the world that you will seek help from the outside out of sheer desperation. This is the great danger that you now face.

No race intervening in the world today is here to help humanity. They are competing races here, competing for advantage in this world, a world of great opportunity and wealth. You do not even realize how important it is.

Your freedom will have to be very practical in the future and very united. You will have to be free together, not free apart from each other. You will have to be free in purpose, not free to break that purpose down. You will have to be free to unite, not free to break that unity.

Perhaps this does not look like freedom to you from where you stand at this moment, but in contrast to the reality of most nations in this entire region of space, it is a great freedom, we assure you.

In our Briefings, we will describe what freedom can look like as it is established. The outer reality of the Greater Community will determine to a greater degree how this freedom will be established and must be maintained.

Yet you still live thinking you are in isolation in the universe, that the universe is a big empty space around you. And perhaps you feel that you are special and blessed by the Divine, so special that any race that would come here would seek to help you, to understand you, or to appreciate you. But such is the ignorance of living in isolation, an ignorance that all emerging races in the universe will likely have, to one degree or another.

Alone you think you are unique and special. But when you enter this grand panorama of life, you will see that others will only regard you for their own benefit, and that the few free races in your part of space will be the only ones who will value you for greater reasons and for higher purposes.

We have had to struggle greatly to regain our freedom from Intervention and to sustain it, which has required us to remain very discreet in this larger panorama of life. It has required that we stay out of the great networks of trade and be free of the overarching organizations of trade that determine how races will participate and engage in commerce with one another. For once you enter these networks, your freedom will be lost.

You who seek greater technology from greater powers in the universe must learn this great lesson. Do not accept any technology from those visiting your world. For they will plant the seeds of your future dependence and with these seeds, as they grow, they will gain greater and greater authority over your minds and your world.

We have had to learn these lessons in our respective worlds. And though our worlds are unique and do not actively engage with each other, except on a very limited basis politically, there are Higher Powers in the universe who direct the great Network of the Wise—who engage individuals in different worlds and nations.

We are part of this Network, and that is why we have come to give you great assistance. We have no interest in establishing ourselves in this world, for you are not ready for Contact. You must gain freedom through your own efforts. We can give you wisdom, warning and perspective, but it is you who must earn your present and future freedom and utilize the great understanding we are giving to you.

You have no idea how daunting the universe really is—how many worlds have fallen under foreign domination, worlds in a very similar state of emergence such as your own, and how few have been able to escape this domination.

It is in part the work of the Higher Powers to support this freedom in races that show potential for it—Higher Powers assigned by the Divine to protect Knowledge in the universe—greater wisdom, purpose and meaning.

Otherwise, advancing technological societies end up becoming ever more like one another: secular, rigid, dominating, competing with each other constantly for advantage. They would not value your individual freedom, but only see you as being chaotic and destructive to your world. They do not understand the things that we speak of. They do not know of the Higher Powers. And if they do have an awareness of this, they will seek to suppress the expression of these Powers wherever they can.

This is the reality of life in the universe, the reality of Separation from the Divine Presence and Purpose—Separation under which you live constantly as well. To break the chains of Separation requires unique wisdom, power and strength, which you must cultivate and which must be supported in you from Higher Powers.

When we speak of Higher Powers, we are not speaking of races of beings in the physical dimension, for there are no enlightened races in the universe, really, only small groups of wisdom connected with each other, through both physical and mysterious means. In this way, the Networks of the Wise can communicate through the Unseen Powers, the Angelic Presence, without ever having physical contact, which in so many cases could never occur.

This is humanity's great challenge, the challenge to its freedom and sovereignty in this world. As we continue, we will talk about the meaning of this freedom, the requirements of this freedom and the great strength that must be given to sustain it amongst so many nations who are not free.

It is a great truth in the universe that the Wise must remain hidden to remain wise. This is the great lesson before you now.

# The Importance of Restraint

You must exercise great restraint in the universe. Do not think you can go out and engage with anyone you find to be interesting, or to travel to other races' worlds, or that you will find great meeting places where many races come together for recreation or for social purposes, for that surely is not the case.

We have been able to watch your films depicting life in the universe. Unfortunately, they are grossly incorrect and dangerously misleading. The reality is very different and very sobering.

You will have to exercise great restraint. If you are determined to have advanced technology from other races, they will gain control of you and your world in time. This must be restrained.

If you seek to travel or to seize territory in other places beyond this solar system, you will face great opposition and conflict. You must restrain yourself from seeking these things.

You will not be able to go beyond this solar system to seek another world like your own should you despoil it too greatly, for such worlds are rare and are owned and guarded by others far more powerful than you. You must restrain yourself in wanting or expecting these things.

If you think that there are other worlds waiting for your exploration should you destroy this one through war or degradation, you will find that you have not the power or the influence in the Greater Community to gain access to them nor a means of reaching them, given your current state of technological development. You must restrain yourself from thinking these things—thinking that another world will be there for the taking, for that will not be the case.

You may think you can despoil your world and that technology will save you from the consequences, but your world will undermine human civilization if you do this and weaken you to the point where you will not be able to resist foreign intervention or the promises of peace, power and technology, which even today are being presented to leaders of your nations and certain leaders of your religious institutions.

You must restrain yourself from thinking you can despoil this world and have any hope of freedom and sovereignty in the universe or think that you can carry on war or competition, destructive competition, for the advantage of your nation. For this will only lead to greater weakness in the human family—fracturing the human family even more, destroying even further the possibility for future cooperation, which will be so necessary for your future and well-being.

You must restrain these notions that war is advantageous for you, that it will gain you profit or advantage here, for it will only sow the seeds of your demise and empower those races who seek to establish themselves here as overlords of this world.

Turn your eyes to the heavens. Your future and your destiny are there. Look up in the sky at night and know that it is full of intelligent life. While there are countless barren and uninhabitable worlds there, the number of races in your local universe in this sector, which is a small region of space, is tremendous. For you live in a very well inhabited part of the galaxy, where rules of engagement have been long established and where war has been suppressed. This is both an advantage and a disadvantage for you. As we have spoken of in our previous Briefings, you are protected from outright conquest, but the possibility and the reality of intervention and persuasion are tremendous.

You will have to gain greater skill here and preparation: awareness, determination, skill, restraint. For you now, the universe is merely the background to your great problems on Earth. But the reality of this universe is the greater force driving your world and your evolution. It is driving you because of the great challenge it presents, and the great opportunity and requirement for unity and cooperation that it will foster if it can be seen and known and responded to.

Never before has Intervention of this nature occurred in the world, for you were still too primitive and your technology still too undeveloped for you to be viable candidates for foreign control and persuasion. Though the world has been visited many times over the course of your long history, Intervention of this kind has never really been attempted.

But now you have created international communication, planetary commerce, planetary trade. You have created a basic infrastructure that others can use and profit from. This, plus the awareness that humanity may grow too strong for Intervention, has generated the Intervention in your world today, accelerated since the last great world conflict, and now accelerating in many different areas of your life.

It is a challenge, if seen correctly, that will enable you to rise above conflict and constant dissension within your world. For the resources of every nation must be united to protect this world out of sheer necessity.

Your understanding of the universe must change and become realistic. Your recognition of your precarious situation must be recognized and become foundational for you.

You must protect the environment of this world—its climate, its resources—or you will fall into poverty and despair on a level never seen before in this world. Yet such things have happened countless times in the universe, with inevitable and predictable results.

Our cultures are old enough to have a history of local events in this part of the galaxy. We have been able to see and know things that you cannot yet see or know directly. We can only give you this wisdom, this greater perspective. Do not think that it is merely a perspective, for it is the truth of your reality. It is what is coming. It is what is here already.

# Freedom in the Universe

Now we will give you a perspective on what freedom looks like once it is established. To be free, a world has to have a united government. It may have representatives from different groups and regions of a world, but it must be a united government. It cannot be a patchwork of warring tribes or even great nations, for that will only invite intervention and manipulation.

The nations that are free foster individual creativity and the value of Knowledge within the individual, but this Knowledge has to be directed where it can serve the greater interests of the world and not merely the preoccupations of the individual. True talent here is highly recognized and valued, but it must be directed. It is not merely the providence of the individual. It is part of the wealth of the nation.

Unlike unfree nations where people's lives are simply catalogued and directed, where individual talent is rarely utilized, where stature in society is based upon family lineage or regional needs alone, in the free nations the individual is valued, and their skills and their wisdom are cultivated because this wisdom and skill are needed for the stability and well-being of the world. They are sent to serve where they can be of the greatest benefit. But it is based upon the need of the whole, not merely the desires of the individual.

A world of errant individuals will never be able to establish freedom in the Greater Community. Here individuality must serve, but it serves according to the individual, and this is one of the things that distinguishes a free nation from a nation that is not free.

In a free nation, dissension is tolerated but only to a certain point. If there is constant rebellion, the nation can never be stable; it can never assume a greater mantle of freedom to even protect the freedoms that it offers its citizens. It must have this stability and this security from the outside.

You do not yet realize you are living in the Greater Community and are subject to its influences, so perhaps this seems very different to you from where you stand at this moment. But it is something you must begin to understand and to entertain. To be a united force, there must be an understanding of the great need that requires this freedom and a willingness to participate and even to sacrifice certain personal freedoms for its sake.

The freedom that you now enjoy is largely only to serve the whims or the desires of the individual, but in the Greater Community this is not what freedom means.

Free societies must maintain their native resources as much as possible and only engage in commerce with other free nations for essential things. Therefore, the plundering of their worlds cannot happen, cannot be allowed if there is to be any stability and security going forward.

There must be great restraint here. For wisdom always requires great restraint. And freedom always means you must be aware of those things you are really not free to do.

It is the freedom of the world. It is the freedom of the whole nation of the world that secures the rights of individuals in the Greater Community. But these rights will be limited out of necessity.

For free nations to remain free, they must be able to thwart or resist all the temptations that will be placed upon them, especially if their worlds are seen to be valuable to others. Here you must see that freedom is seen as a great threat to the unfree nations. They are afraid the freedoms that the free nations have may influence their own populations in some way, leading to rebellion, discontent and dissension.

Such things as art and music and dance that you enjoy today would be seen as a great threat to the cultures that are not free. Individual freedoms that the free nation can give its citizens would be seen as a threat to those nations that are not free.

As a consequence, free nations do not broadcast out into the universe. They do not reveal what life is like in their worlds, if they can avoid it. They do not engage in larger networks of trade, which are always very controlling and manipulative and make one's own world vulnerable to the powers of persuasion on a far greater scale.

Free nations must be largely self-sufficient here. They must be very united. And they must be very discreet. These are the three great requirements of freedom in the universe. And you cannot escape them. There are no exceptions here.

The free nations, being discreet, do not travel around the universe seeking to plant their flags or to exert their influence or seek to intervene in the affairs of others. They may promote freedom and responsibility, as we are doing through these Briefings, but they do not intervene. For to intervene is to transgress one's own discretion. To intervene is to make yourself known in the larger universe, and free nations do not want to do this. Their insulation is critical to their unique accomplishments.

In the free nations, the power of Knowledge in the individual is valued and supported, even within the restraints of their society. In unfree nations, this is either unknown or brutally suppressed. And the gatherings of the Wise in unfree nations must occur in great secrecy in order to survive, which is often the case.

People of your world think the universe must be better than the world itself—more elevated, more free, more spiritual, more ethical—to be sought, to be encouraged, to be invited into this world. This is perhaps the normal expectation of races living in isolation. Such was the same in our worlds until our emergence into the Greater Community began and we had to face Intervention.

We are telling you these things because you must understand what the journey of freedom really is about. It is not about individual happiness. It is about the freedom of your race. It is not about individual pursuits or indulgences. It is about the stability and security of your world. Freedom here is not a right in the universe. It is a great privilege and a great accomplishment that must be earned earnestly and consistently and protected against all challenges.

You cannot have a romantic view of life in the universe if you hope to survive within it. Such is the great sobriety that wisdom brings. Do not have fanciful notions about the value of Contact or what other races can teach you about freedom through their intervention in your world, for that is a fatal error, and a tragic one at that.

We know, through the Networks of the Wise, how much has been given to this world to sustain and support the threads of freedom and wisdom that still exist here. Much has been invested in your world for this purpose. Even as you escalate and progress in your technological development, there is great emphasis on your world for its potential here, its potential to be a free race in the universe, a potential that you must seize upon and develop through your own will and cooperation with one another.

We cannot give you this freedom, and there is no other race in the universe who can give you this freedom, nor come here and establish it for you. Any race that promises this is truly deceiving you and is here for other purposes, their own purposes.

It is, however, to our benefit to have another free race within this sector of space. We would welcome that, though we seek no formal relations. You are not ready for formal relations. And you may not be ready for a long time to come. You are not strong enough. You are not united enough. You are not mature enough, still indulging yourself in conflict and war and destructive competition.

If we can support the emergence of Knowledge in worlds such as yours, we will do that according to the dictates of the Divine, through the Networks of Knowledge, not through the networks of governments. Even our own governments do not know what we are doing here. Though they would support it in theory, it is not wise for them to have this knowledge, for then they would have to be responsible for our actions.

For in most cases, free nations have had to make non-intervention agreements with the larger nations around them in order to keep these larger nations out of the free nations' sphere and activities. We are contravening this in our small presence in service to your world. For we are governed by Higher Powers, of which you know little about, but of which you must become educated, and we will speak of this next.

# Higher Powers

There are two realities in the universe; one overlaps the other. The first and most primary in your experience is the reality of Separation and evolutionary change, planetary change—from primitive life, primitive social organizations, early nations, larger nations, world nations and finally emergence into a Greater Community of larger nations.

Overlapping this is the work of the Divine throughout the universe, carried out by the Higher Powers, the Angelic Forces that oversee all races, even in the unfree nations, looking for opportunities to cultivate Knowledge in individuals who are free enough and able enough to respond. This creates a great Network of the Wise, which then can support the emergence of free nations, who still have the potential for this great accomplishment.

In the physical universe, there are only the forces that were set in motion at the beginning of time. There is no Divine Plan organizing everything, controlling everything, for the physical universe is largely chaotic and governed by celestial forces, geologic forces and, within worlds where life has been able to take hold, biological forces. That was all set in motion at the beginning of time by the Divine, and it is running itself now.

The Divine Intervention is through the Higher Powers, through the Networks of the Wise and through nations that have been able to keep individual awareness and Knowledge alive, despite all of the hazards and conflict that usually exist in a world's evolution and social development.

As we have said, there are no enlightened races in the universe that we are aware of, but there are free races, and within free races, the Wise may guide their nations. They would be more plentiful than they would ever be in nations that are not free.

The Divine has outposts in many, many places. And there are groups of the Wise working in many, many places, even in great secrecy. Free nations allow these groups to resurface and become effective in society. But the truly Wise are individuals networked in small groups, networked within their own nation or networked between nations, connected through the Higher Powers.

So do not think that there is an enlightened race who is going to come and enlighten humanity, or that humanity itself is going to become an enlightened race. That is far beyond its capabilities. But to be a free race where Knowledge can be fostered and supported openly, that is the great achievement. That is the great challenge and requirement placed before you now.

There are two kinds of freedom. There is practical freedom to live your life without overdue restraint or domination, practical freedom to live with stability and security, without the constant threat of war or overbearing corruption. This is the foundational freedom, and it is so very important. It is the first thing that must be established.

Then there is the greater spiritual freedom of the individual to begin their return to the Divine and to gain access to the deeper Knowledge that God has created in all individuals, in all races in the universe who are living in Separation in physical reality.

This greater freedom is the calling of individuals, and it is limited by the fundamental freedoms they may have in their respective worlds and cultures. But the greater freedom is the ultimate freedom because the Power of Heaven can move through these individuals in service to others and, through the great Networks of the Wise, foster freedom and Knowledge in the entire Greater Community.

You must understand that the Work of the Divine in your world is connected to the Work of the Divine in all worlds. There is no special plan for your world, which is but a tiny place in a greater universe. God's Plan is unified and well established. And Knowledge lives within you as an individual, which is how you connect with the Divine Presence and Power and how you begin to gain your inner freedom, even beyond the restraints of your outer environment.

Wherever the fundamental freedom can be built and established and maintained over time represents a greater possibility for the higher freedom to be fostered and supported, and the greater freedom that it will have in its expression in that world, in that nation, in that culture. For freedom in the universe is not the freedom to further your Separation. It is the freedom to return to your Source and to be of service in this physical reality.

As you can see here, even your most fundamental notions of peace, freedom and responsibility must now be redefined within a larger context, or you will continue to think that your peace and your freedom and your responsibility are for yourself alone, or for your family alone. This is not what these things mean in the Greater Community, and these will not be effective or even meaningful in the world you are now beginning to enter, where environmental degradation, the loss of food production and the changing climate of your world will make life much more difficult, requiring greater participation and cooperation if you are to succeed.

Even those things that threaten you from the outside, where they can undermine you here in this world, can foster greater freedom in the truest sense if this opportunity is recognized and claimed by enough people. The greater the challenge, the greater the opportunity.

For right now humanity is far too weak, far too divided, far too disorganized to ever be able to sustain itself as a free and sovereign race in the universe. What will build this strength, this cooperation, this freedom and this responsibility are the great challenges facing you now: the challenge of degradation and collapse from within and the challenge of Intervention and subjugation from without. Only these great and overbearing challenges will generate the requirement for freedom, strength and responsibility that we speak of here.

Not everyone will be able to respond to this challenge, but even if a small minority of people in your world can do this, it can lead to a greater outcome. The world is governed by small numbers of people, for better or worse. In this case, a small number of people could save the entire human race from collapse and disintegration.

Yes, it is a tremendous challenge. Yes, it seems to be unfair to your understanding. It even seems cruel to your understanding. But this is what it means to grow up in the universe: to become a mature race and not an adolescent race that fights and struggles amongst itself for privilege and wealth and opportunity.

We have had to grow up under the pain and challenge of Intervention and the degradation of our worlds. It is part of life, becoming an adult, becoming responsible, not only for oneself but for the well-being of one's world—driven now by necessity, driven now by challenge, driven now by great threat. All these things are the foundation for the strength, the wisdom, the cooperation that you will need for the great change that is coming for the world.

We therefore do not bring peace, as you think of it. We bring challenge. We bring responsibility. We bring clarity. We bring wisdom. We bring strength. We bring the calling for all these things.

If you could but see or have a sense for where your life is heading and the degree of Intervention in your world today, it will either defeat you or you will rise to meet it. Such is the unseen opportunity here.

God knows this is the greatest threshold for the human family, the greatest threshold you have ever faced and may ever face—a declining world and emergence into the Greater Community, which usually accompany each other. God has sent a New Message into the world. We know of this. That is part of what has called us here to encourage the human family. We will speak of this next, for it is fundamental to your success and to your freedom.

# The Great Coordination

We are aware that a great Revelation is being sent to the world. Though we have not been given this Revelation ourselves, we are connected to it. It is because God has asked us to do this through the Networks of the Wise, to take this promising world of yours and give it wisdom, encouragement, strength and purpose that it must have now to overcome its tendencies and to prepare for its challenging future.

As we were aided in gaining our freedom in our own worlds, at different times and different situations, it is incumbent upon us to aid you in a similar manner, for this is one of the ways that wisdom and strength are shared in the universe. It is a long lineage. We know not of its ancient history, yet we are part of its expression.

Our coming to you with these Briefings is connected to this Revelation for the world. So fortunate you are to have a Revelation from God for the world. There are so few worlds in the universe where this could ever take place in any kind of public way. In a free nation, it is possible and does occur, but it is still very rare.

We do not know of all that this Revelation will speak of, but we do know that it is part of your preparation for the things that we speak of. We know that it is a gift of strength and empowerment for humanity.

Yet we are called to bear witness to the realities of life in the universe and the meaning of the things that we speak of here, things of the utmost importance to you and to your future. It is all part of a Greater Coordination to bring to humanity this great promise and great assistance.

We are far from your world now, so we cannot witness what is occurring. Yet we are still part of this Greater Coordination. This is what we are committed to in our small group, those of us who still remain.

We understand that there is a Messenger for this great Revelation, and it is to this Messenger we were directed to send the Briefings from the Allies of Humanity. Our contact with him was made possible by the Higher Powers, contact made in such a way that it could not be interfered with or traced by any technological means.

It is part of the way the Divine works in the universe to foster wisdom, freedom and Knowledge wherever that is possible and to whatever extent it is possible. We can only pray, in the way that we pray, that this great Revelation may meet and reach enough people in your world to have its full benefit and impact.

This fulfills our task, which is to speak of these things that we speak of and to bring you Wisdom and Knowledge from the universe that we have had to learn through great trial and great necessity.

We understand this will be very confusing to many people, all these things we speak of here now. And we did not speak of the Revelation from God before because we felt it would be too much for people to try to comprehend, along with everything we are charged with expressing, the wisdom we are charged to give to you.

But now that we are far away, we can speak of other matters. It is necessary that we be a witness to this, to this Revelation from the Divine that you are so fortunate to have in your midst. If only you could see how fortunate you are, given what freedom you have today, which has been the product of so much human giving and sacrifice already. If you could understand how rare an event this is, your gratitude would be overflowing, and you would understand its great importance.

We must again speak of the reality of freedom from where we stand and what we know, for we are asked to bear witness to these things from our experience, not merely from our ideology or the way that we think of these things. We know that freedom is not a right in the universe. It is a rare and precious thing. It must be established and secured with the greatest determination.

We have earned the freedom to serve in this way, to be able to serve another race in this way—in a way that the people of your world can hear, that it can be made available as testimony. How rare this is indeed.

We have been assisted in this way once we were able to se- cure our freedom in our nations, for the Greater Powers have been able to serve us directly. For the development of freedom and the stability of freedom is an ongoing challenge that requires great maturity, wisdom and restraint. Though we are not enlightened societies as you would think of them perhaps, we are free enough to have this opportunity and to be served in this way.

But humanity does not yet have this freedom, even at present, for a new Revelation for your world will be greatly resisted and contested. It is the evolution of your race as a whole that makes this so.

Yet as you stand at the threshold of life in the universe, you could not have a greater advantage or a greater strength being given to you. For as we have said repeatedly, no race will come and establish freedom for you. No race will come and elevate your technology for you. No race will come and manage your world for you. Not for you. This is the truth that must be recognized, or you will not understand what you are facing.

It is so rare that one race can serve another in the ways that we are doing here, for usually the avenues of support are very secretive, very subtle, beyond the surveillance of governments. It is a very precious thing that we speak of.

Regarding free societies, there is something else we must tell you. The free societies recognize the limits of beneficial technology. Should you take technology too far, beyond your basic needs, beyond the basic benefits to your society, you draw other powers to you. Your insulation in the universe begins to diminish. Now you are left with powers that are very difficult to conceal.

For even though our races are free in the ways that we have spoken of, there are still other eyes watching us at all times. Should we demonstrate any extraordinary abilities or extraordinary technology, it will invite greater and greater scrutiny and persuasion. Others will seek to gain it from us by whatever means, short of outright conquest. That is why the powers we might have must be expressed very subtly, even kept out of the public view amongst the Wise who guide our worlds.

This is the truth of life in the universe that greater power, greater strength and its demonstrations must be hidden if you seek to have the opportunity for freedom and self-determination.

There are seers in other nations who try to see into our affairs, who try to discern what we are doing, what we have, our strengths and our weaknesses. We can only counteract this to a certain degree. For once the eyes of the universe are set upon you, they will continue to watch. Either through technological means or by more subtle means, this would be the case.

So the Wise that govern our worlds do not share all the things they know with the public, for the public is not strong enough to maintain this with discretion. That is too much to ask of a whole race. You who think freedom is the freedom to know everything have no idea what you are thinking or the meaning of this amongst the presence of greater forces.

Therefore, understand that beyond meeting the real authentic needs of a race, technology should not go any further. It gives you powers you cannot use and must hide. It opens discernment from the outside and invites intervention and manipulation and ever-greater scrutiny. Therefore, do not think that endlessly developing technology is a worthy and noble pursuit. It is only beneficial in certain ways, to a certain point. Beyond this, it creates danger and hazard.

Should you have a power of insight or a power of technology that other nations do not have, they will seek it from you. This is why the Wise must remain hidden, a great and enduring truth in the universe.

With power comes this responsibility, this discretion, this discernment, this caution, this being very careful with one's mind and action and thought in light of their impact upon others and what they may invite from the outside. We in our group were all students of this great Teaching, which you now have an opportunity to learn out of sheer necessity.

Our free nations must be preoccupied with stability and security, for free nations do not co-exist well with large nations that are not free, larger nations that are more powerful technologically and militarily. We must guard not only our borders but our thoughts. This is the burden of the Wise in all places.

We understand that the New Revelation for the world can teach people these things and give this to the human family. If this is true, then that is a very great sign.

It is possible that there may be those amongst you who become truly wise with this. Your task is to secure the freedom of your people and your world, to keep Knowledge alive in your world, to keep wisdom alive in your world, where it will always seem to be under threat and attacked by others who want to use everything for personal power and benefit. It is a truth in your world as much as it is a truth in the Greater Community. Everything we are telling you here today is a truth in your world, for it is a truth everywhere. It is a truth in the realm of Separation.

We bring with this great and sober teaching encouragement, for the human family has great potential. The awareness of the Divine, and the power of Knowledge in the individual, has not been obliterated in your world. It has not been forgotten. It is still valued by many, and in some parts of your world, it is still practiced by many. This is a great sign in the universe, where very few advancing races have this kind of potential.

We know that Knowledge within you can respond to these things and resonate because it is a greater realm of truth, because within your life you were meant to be part of the Greater Coordination as well. Though it seems like a distant possibility to you now, perhaps, it is foundational to who you are and why you are in the world at this time, for it alone holds the strength and the vision and the resonance that can enable you to respond and to perceive your situation correctly and beneficially. It will call you out of an ordinary and disappointing life into a far greater realm of service and meaning, as it has done for us.

We cannot yet return to our home worlds until our mission is complete. It has taken many years for this to take place, even so far. There have been many challenges and setbacks. We have lost members of our group. We have had to escape to distant and safe havens. For the Intervention that is participating in your world became aware of us after our first set of Briefings was delivered, and their search for us began. We do not think they were expecting our presence and surely would be challenged and threatened by our message.

Yet our mission is not yet complete, for though we are no longer in your vicinity, there is Wisdom from the universe we can still provide for you. You need this Wisdom now, and you will need it ever increasingly as you go forward.

# The Networks of the Wise

Our purpose is not religion, for religion has many faces in the universe. There are many religions that we have heard of and a few we have encountered indirectly beyond our own shores.

It is not our purpose, you see, for we are guided by the Higher Powers, which you would consider to be the Angelic Assembly. Because our worlds are relatively free in the universe, our religions reflect the things that we study for the benefit of our races and for the well-being of our worlds. But what we ourselves study is of a greater nature. It is of the Coordination of the Wise, connected with Higher Powers beyond the physical realm.

Therefore, we are not here to represent the religions of our world, for we are functioning very independently of them. We are not here to represent the races of our world, as if we were ambassadors of some kind, for we are here on a very different kind of errand and mission. We are not here to establish formal relations between our nations and your nation because it is way too soon for anything like that to be established. And that is really not our ultimate goal. For we have been directed for a greater purpose than this.

Religion in the universe is so often an emblem of the governing powers, if it exists at all. We feel it is quite rare that greater spiritual truth exists in any race. We find it almost unimaginable that there could be an enlightened race, for that is too much to expect of those living in the physical reality.

But the Wise have many associates and a greater Network, acting independently of governments and large commercial institutions and great trading networks. These things may be useful to us, but for the most part, we function beyond them. You will find the Wise in many places, but usually hidden, functioning in deep secrecy. For to have such greater power in the universe would, in most cases, seem threatening to the ruling powers of any world, unless they be very free in the ways that we speak of here today.

To be governed by Higher Powers from afar in service to the Divine can only be the providence of very select individuals, individuals not just selected because they have great stature in their worlds. No, it is of a different nature than this.

The Networks of the Wise are chosen from a greater history of individuals, a greater destiny that they have. It is a difficult thing because to have such a great destiny, particularly in a world that is not free, represents a very arduous task, a very dangerous task, a task that requires tremendous restraint and discretion and discernment.

Do not think of this as some joyful journey that you hope to be selected to take, for in the universe at large, it is a daunting task and a great responsibility. And even should you meet the requirements over time and be chosen for this kind of role, you would have to be connected with other individuals whom you would never meet, even within your own world per se, and within other worlds as well.

You would have to wait for them for long periods of time for certain situations to emerge and to become fruitful and appropriate for your work. So this would require immense patience as well. That is why we can be so patient with the human family, for we have had to develop this great patience, even with one another in the Great Coordination.

Our mission is not yet complete. When it is, we will return to our worlds, if we can survive this process. When this could happen we cannot tell, but we are being held as a vital resource for the human family—to be called upon when needed, to bear witness to life in the universe as we know it and have experienced it, and the greater truths that we have had to learn and that our races have had to learn—things that the human family cannot see or know without this testimony.

It is wisest for you now to simply have an open mind and set aside the kind of cultural beliefs there may be regarding life beyond your world, to not be influenced by others' opinions, or the works of your governments, or the fantasies and speculation that exist around this great and important subject.

The human family, without even knowing it, is part of a Greater Coordination. It is something only the Wise can fully understand. And even here their comprehension of this great Network must remain incomplete. For what individual can know of a Network so vast, so complicated and coordinated from Higher and Greater Powers, subject to so many circumstances and changing conditions that it is beyond the capacity of any individual, or even group, to fully realize? But to know you are part of this Coordination, to carry out your duties as part of this Coordination, that is the mountain you must climb to learn of these things sufficiently.

We speak of things now in service to the Revelation that is being given to the world, and its teaching about life in the universe in particular. For you must have testimony from the universe itself, and not from one race or individual alone, but from a greater Network representing countless races that function beyond the reach of governments and commerce; beyond the reach of ambitious individuals and groups and nations; beyond all of the corruption and manipulation that exist in this region of space, which is considerable and complicated and dangerous.

We bring to you the reality of life in the universe as we see it and have known it. It is not simply our understanding, however, that we present to you here. It is the wisdom of the Networks of the Wise, who share their wisdom with one another through the Higher Powers. In this way, Heaven has its agents on the ground—here, there, everywhere, hidden, small groups and sometimes isolated individuals, but very well connected so that the wisdom that we provide can not only represent our individual experience or understanding, but the wisdom of the Wise throughout this part of the universe.

There is no race that could understand the meaning of life fully in this universe, or understand fully that all beings living in the physical reality are living in a state of Separation from the Divine.

The Revelation for your world now, and the Messenger sent for this purpose, can explain these things to you, for you need a human representative to do this for you. He too is part of the Greater Coordination, as is his family. They have been sent here as the seeds of the Greater Coordination in the world, not only to meet the great challenge of Intervention and the great challenges that humanity is facing, but also to accompany humanity's emergence into the Greater Community and to build this sacred bond here.

For if humanity is to ever attain real freedom in the universe, or be able to maintain this freedom and to attain stability in this world with your environment, you will need this Greater Coordination here to maintain a higher level of Knowledge and, if possible, even to advise your future leaders. For in a free nation, what leader would not want to have access to such great wisdom without being part of the Network itself? For those in political power are rarely involved in the great Networks because they are too heavily controlled and influenced by their governments.

Therefore, do not think that the notable people in your world are part of this greater Network. They are not free. They are not able to function at this level. But those who are part of these Networks can advise them into the future. And such advice in a free nation would be critically important because now you have access to wisdom from the whole universe, not just from local regions, not just from individual perceptions, not just from one nation's own history and limited awareness.

We say these things to you so that you may understand more completely who we are and why we are here and what we serve. We hope this will dispel any notion that we are here representing political powers or economic powers or any power associated with the Intervention. We are not here to represent other governments, other worlds.

Even the free nations cannot intervene in your world, and would not, for this would contravene their non-intervention agreements in the universe, which most free nations must establish to have autonomy in this larger arena of life.

It is important, because you are an emerging race, that you may know of the great Networks. Even though the Intervention may hear this information, they cannot gain access to these great Networks. Only the great Networks that are free of the machinations of physical life and governance could have such freedom in the universe.

That is why any individual group in the Network will only have a partial understanding so that even if they were to fail or to be overtaken by other powers, they could not betray the entirety of the Network.

That is why perhaps you, who are hearing this and receiving this message, must come to understand that ever-greater wisdom, ever-greater awareness, is not the goal. Beyond the functionality of your true role and purpose, Heaven will not give you this because it would make others far too vulnerable to your mistakes. Great care is brought here in the development of individuals and the assignment of roles.

As we have watched your world when we were in its proximity, there are others who watch over us to make sure we do not err. For all beings in the universe are fallible and prone to error. Such is the condition of living in Separation in physical form. We are in physical form. We are sentient beings from several worlds. Therefore, the Higher Powers watch over us far more carefully than they would over other individuals.

But we still can falter. We still can be overtaken by other powers who seek to gain access to us or to destroy us or who perceive us as a threat. That is why we are not in your world, walking your world, you see, because there are powers within your world who would perceive us as a threat, most assuredly—threatening their political power or their religious position, for we represent a Greater Authority in life.

We are not mere servants. We are emissaries of this Greater Authority. But our mission here is very specific, as we have stated in our Briefings. We understand the limits of these responsibilities, which in and of themselves are great enough to challenge us continuously.

Therefore, it is important for you to understand that there are two levels of governance in the universe. There is the governance of political and religious powers and economic powers, which seem to predominate everywhere and must even be strong in free worlds. This is the image of the universe that your senses report.

But there is a greater level of governance and influence that speaks to the deepest part of you, which we call Knowledge, or the Septa Varne. This greater influence and power speaks to this within you and calls certain individuals into higher levels of service in their respective worlds. And those who can succeed in this long preparation will become linked to this Greater Coordination of the Divine, whose Will and Purpose is to establish freedom and wisdom and the power of Knowledge everywhere, for its potential exists in all sentient beings in all worlds throughout the universe.

Though we serve a specific function to alert and help prepare humanity for its emergence into this Greater Community of life, we also represent this Greater Authority and influence, and speak, if we can, to the emergence of Knowledge in the individual as we have done, in support of the great Revelation that the Divine has sent to the world—a rare and remarkable event in this part of the universe. For how few races in this part of the universe could receive in public a New Revelation from God. You have no idea how fortunate you are to be in this position, or how rare it is in a universe of oppressed nations and strict governments.

You who seem fascinated and in love with technology do not yet realize its great hazards and the risk it poses to your freedom, individually and as a whole world. That is why we have said in the Briefings not to receive technology from other races, for this plants the seed of their control in your world—so that they will control your world more than you, and you will become dependent upon their technology.

Do not think that great technology in the universe represents spiritual power in any way. This is entirely false. Do not think this represents real spiritual power in your own world, for the very same reasons we speak of. We must echo this Wisdom that we are sure is part of the great Revelation being given to the world.

There must be great sobriety in entering this universe. It is the greatest threshold that any one world can undergo. It has great hazards and can have great promise, depending on what is fostered in that world and the degree to which the deeper Knowledge has been cultivated and kept alive there.

Humanity is seen to have great promise in this regard, but there are great forces in your world that work against this and have always worked against this and there is the great vulnerability for humanity to the universe—to its influences, to its seductions, to its promises of peace and power, to its offerings of technology to a more primitive and yet more spiritually oriented race such as your own.

Therefore, understand that the true Allies of Humanity are only in part representatives of the free nations. Yet its full meaning indicates that it is the Network of the Wise that is your greatest ally and asset, and those who can represent this in reality, for they will be free of the corruption of any world. They do not have technological power. They use technology to serve their ends, but that is not their force. That is not their strength. That is not their banner. For they have no banner, being largely invisible to your eyes.

Humanity's true Allies, then, are the Wise in all worlds and the few who are Wise in your world who will foster the power of Knowledge. But your greatest ally is the Unseen Ones, the Higher Powers, what you would think of as the Angelic, who are now bringing a New Revelation from the Divine into the world to prepare humanity for the Greater Community, to provide the foundation for true unity and greater freedom in your world.

We have been called into service and coordination with the presentation of this great Revelation. Though it has not been given to us specifically, we know of its purpose and its intent, and we echo its Wisdom most assuredly. But what must be taught for you within your world must come from within your world. And what must be taught to you from beyond the world must come from beyond the world. It is all part of this great Revelation for humanity.

Therefore, we ask that you think of us in this greater way even though it may be hard to understand or to conceive of. It is so important for you to separate and distinguish the Divine Powers at work in the universe from the political powers that exert themselves everywhere.

Never confuse these two, or you will be open to great seduction and manipulation. Never think that another nation who arrives on your shores is spiritually inclined or represents the Networks of the Wise, for that would be the ultimate form of seduction for your people. And though the Intervention will try to promote this idea, being aware of your predispositions and your vulnerabilities, you must not succumb to such persuasions.

Never think that those who seem to have amazing technology are in any way elevated above you in their ethics or morality or spirituality. You have seen the truth of this in your own world this past century, most assuredly, that greater technology does not represent greater truth, greater meaning or greater purpose.

There is so much that must be distinguished and discerned here for you to understand our message, our purpose and our reality. There are so many ideas and beliefs that must be set aside consciously to be able to see these things with any degree of clarity. It is a challenge in your world and in all worlds.

How few in the universe have the freedom to see without the overwhelming influence of their nations and cultures and religions, if they have a religion. It is a rare and beautiful thing, and the potential for this exists within each person in the world, within you and others because Knowledge has been kept alive here through the great efforts of many servants of the Divine, operating at different levels, at great sacrifice of individuals, great courage, great integrity—things which seem rare, but are still present enough in your world to give your race as a whole a greater promise and recognition amongst the Wise.

May our gifts to you then resonate deeply. And may you recognize the requirements and the restraint necessary in order to see a Greater Reality that lives within your midst at all times and throughout the universe.

# 12-POINT SUMMARY OF
# THE ALLIES OF HUMANITY BRIEFINGS

To assist you in sharing The Allies' Message and Briefings with others, we are including this 12-point summary of the four sets of Briefings. This summary represents only a general overview and does not include many of the important details which make complete comprehension of the Allies Briefings possible. Visit www.alliesofhumanity.org for a downloadable version to share with others.

1.  Humanity's destiny is to emerge into and to engage with a Greater Community of intelligent life in the universe.

2.  Contact with other forms of intelligent life represents the greatest threshold that humanity has ever faced. The results of this Contact will determine humanity's future for generations to come. This Contact is happening now.

3.  Humanity is unprepared for Contact. Researchers are still unable to clearly see who is visiting our world and why. Governments are not revealing what they know, and most people are still in denial that this phenomenon is even occurring.

4.  Because of this lack of preparation, humanity's true Allies sent representatives to a location near Earth to observe the extraterrestrial presence and activities within our world. The Allies of Humanity Briefings represent their report.

5. The Briefings reveal that our world is undergoing an extraterrestrial Intervention by forces who, as demonstrated by their actions, are here to subvert human authority and to integrate into human societies for their own advantage. These forces represent non-military organizations who are here to seek human and biological resources. The Allies refer to these forces as the "Collectives." The Collectives do not value human freedom.

6. Because the Intervention is being carried out by small groups of intervening forces, it must rely primarily upon deception and persuasion to achieve its goals. The Allies Briefings describe in detail how this is being accomplished and what we must do to stop it.

7. This extraterrestrial Intervention is being focused in four arenas:

   • It is influencing certain individuals in positions of power and authority in government, commerce and religion to cooperate with the Intervention through the promise of greater wealth, power and technology

   • It is creating hidden establishments in the world from which the Intervention can exert its influence in the mental environment, seeking to make people everywhere open and compliant to its will through a "Pacification Program"

   • It is manipulating our religious values and spiritual impulses in order to gain human allegiance to their cause

   • It is taking people against their will, and often without their awareness, to support an interbreeding program designed to create a hybrid race and a new leadership who would be bonded to the "visitors."

8. Those extraterrestrial visitors who have been potentially beneficial to humanity have all retreated from the world in the face of the Intervention. Those remaining are alien races who are not here for our benefit. This leaves us in an unambiguous situation regarding the intentions and activities of the extraterrestrial presence. This enables us to clearly see what we are dealing with. Otherwise, it would be impossible for us to tell friend from foe.

9. The Allies Briefings emphasize the grave danger in our accepting and becoming reliant upon ET technology offered by the Intervention. This will only lead to our becoming dependent on the "visitors," resulting in our loss of freedom and self-sufficiency. No true ally of humanity would offer this to us. The Allies emphasize that we have earth-based solutions to all the problems that we face. What we lack as a race are unity, will and cooperation.

10. In spite of the great challenge we now face, humanity still has a great advantage if we can respond in time. The Allies Briefings reveal both the Intervention's strengths and its weaknesses. One of the Intervention's weaknesses is its reliance upon human acquiescence and cooperation to achieve its goals. According to Greater Community rules of conduct within the region of space in which our world exists, Intervention is not allowed unless it can be demonstrated that the native people welcome and approve of it. Here our voices can have power in the Greater Community. At this moment, the

Intervention has few critics. But if enough people can become aware of it and speak out against it, the Intervention will be thwarted and must withdraw. This is the first step in humanity's preparation for dealing with the realities of life in the universe. This step and all the steps that follow give humanity its one great chance to overcome its longstanding conflicts and to unite in its own defense for the preservation of the world. The Allies emphasize that we as human beings have the spiritual and collective power to do this, and that we must do this if we want to survive and advance as a free and independent race in the universe.

11.  Preparation for our contact with the Greater Community begins with awareness, education, and Knowledge, our spiritual Mind.

12.  In facing the Greater Community, humanity must build unity, self-sufficiency and discretion. These are the three requirements that all free nations must establish to be free in the universe.

*"If humanity were well versed in Greater Community affairs, you would resist any visitation to your world unless a mutual agreement had been established previously. You would know enough not to allow your world to be so vulnerable."*
THE ALLIES OF HUMANITY, BOOK ONE: THE THIRD BRIEFING

# THE STORY OF THE MESSENGER

**M**arshall Vian Summers may ultimately be recognized as one of the most prophetic figures to emerge in our lifetime. For more than thirty years, he has been quietly writing and teaching a spirituality that acknowledges the undeniable reality that humanity lives in a vast and populated universe and now urgently needs to prepare for the challenge of emerging into a Greater Community of intelligent life.

MV Summers teaches the timeless Knowledge and Wisdom from the Greater Community that are so needed in the world today if humanity is to overcome corruption and conflict and prepare for the Greater Community. His books, *Greater Community Spirituality: A New Revelation* and *Steps to Knowledge: The Book of Inner Knowing*, winner of the Year 2000 Book of the Year Award for Spirituality, together present a new spiritual paradigm that could be considered the first "Theology of Contact." Of the entire body of his work, 20 books have so far been published by New Knowledge Library. These works together represent some of the most original and advanced spiritual teachings to appear in modern history.

Marshall is the Founder of The Society for the New Message, a non-profit 501(c)(3) organization dedicated to bringing into the world a new awareness of humanity's place in the universe. With *The Allies of Humanity Books*, Marshall becomes perhaps the first major figure to sound a clear warning about the real nature of the extraterrestrial Intervention now occurring in the world, calling for personal responsibility, preparation and collective awareness.

His pioneering work, *Life in the Universe*, presents the full scope of his revelation about the nature of life and spirituality across this larger panorama in which we live called the "Greater Community." He has devoted his life to receiving these revelations about the Greater Community and is committed to sharing this "New Message" with as many people as possible.

# THE ALLIES BOOKS
## ONE, TWO AND THREE

## THE ALLIES OF HUMANITY
## BOOK ONE

AN URGENT MESSAGE ABOUT THE
EXTRATERRESTRIAL PRESENCE IN THE
WORLD TODAY

AlliesOfHumanity.org/
BookOne

## CONTENTS

## THE ALLIES OF HUMANITY BOOK TWO

### HUMAN UNITY, FREEDOM & THE HIDDEN REALITY OF CONTACT

### CONTENTS

*The Four Fundamental Questions*
*How the Allies Briefings Came to Be*
*Who are the Allies of Humanity?*
*Allies' Preface to the Second Set of Briefings*

AlliesOfHumanity.org/
BookTwo

### THE ALLIES' BRIEFINGS

### THE TEACHERS' COMMENTARIES

*Who are the Teachers?*

*Message from Marshall Vian Summers*
*A New Hope in the World*

# THE ALLIES OF HUMANITY
# BOOK THREE
## A MESSAGE TO EARTH

## CONTENTS

*Introduction*
*Who are the Allies of Humanity?*

FIRST BRIEFING:       The Reality of
                      Contact
SECOND BRIEFING:      The Requirements
                      for Freedom
THIRD BRIEFING:       The Tools of
                      Intervention
FOURTH BRIEFING:      Hidden Powers
FIFTH BRIEFING:       Many Voices in the Universe
SIXTH BRIEFING:       Greater Community Realities
SEVENTH BRIEFING:     Questions & Answers
FINAL WORDS

AlliesOfHumanity.org/
BookThree

*The Solution*
*There Is a New Hope in the World*
*Resistance and Empowerment: The Ethics of Contact*
*Taking Action—What You Can Do*
*Message from Marshall Vian Summers*

APPENDIX:      *12-Point Summary*
               *Important Terms*
               *Further Study*
               *About MV Summers*
               *Books of the New Message from God*

Lightning Source UK Ltd.
Milton Keynes UK
UKHW011318200522
403286UK00001B/23